Coaching Youth Basketball

Offensive Strategies

By Jordan Lyons

ISBN-13: 9781530822140
ISBN-10: 1530822149

The information in this book is meant to supplement, not replace, proper basketball training. Like any sport involving speed, equipment, balance and environmental factors, basketball poses some inherent risk. The author and publisher advise readers to take full responsibility for their safety and know their limits. Before practicing the skills described in this book, be sure that your equipment is well maintained, and do not take risks beyond your level of experience, aptitude, training, and comfort level.

Cover by Jordan Lyons

Table of Contents

Introduction

I remember one of my first practices as a head youth basketball coach. Since the moment I decided to volunteer for the opportunity, I had been excited to install and test an offense. From my years of playing organized basketball, countless hours running offenses as a point guard, and several seasons of assistant coaching years earlier, I figured it would be cinch to pass on my knowledge to some eager basketball players. Devising what I thought would be an appropriate offense for my fourth and fifth grade team to run (many of which had little experience in organized basketball), I anxiously showed up for our second practice of the year ready to install the offensive set. I explained to them my brilliant strategy and we tried to walk through the offense together. After running it in slow motion for a while, I decided to have them try it full speed. I watched as my team floundered through the set, having almost no idea what they were doing. Part of me knew that offenses take time to learn and master, but you could see the confusion etched on their faces and in their blank eyes was more than unfamiliarity. This wasn't going to be a matter of practicing. It was a completely failure on my part. The confusion wasn't their fault, it was mine.

What I neglected to remember is all the years spent practicing, watching, and learning as well as the patience of coaches who taught me this offense. I had the curse of knowledge. I forgot what it took to get there. Only then did I start to grasp the way forward for my team. It all should have started with developing the right fundamentals to be successful. You need the skills like passing, dribbling, screening, and cutting before you can actually run a play. On top of that, running an efficient offense takes time, patience, and practice. Start with something simple and keep layering on complexity once you get the hang of the simple stuff. Break down the offense into pieces. What I hope this book is able to do for you and your team is to provide a framework that allows you to start with the simple. Furthermore, I hope to also provide a blueprint for how to get from those building block phases to an effective basketball offense.

Before even stepping on to the court, I want to start with an understanding of the game of basketball. That's why you will find the first pages provide an overview of popular basketball terminology. The terms listed there will be littered throughout this book, so it's good to get a grasp of them before moving on. I will also go over the basic positions that your players will typically play. This overview will hopefully prepare you to better under the more advanced parts of this text.

After covering the popular terms, I will layout several "skill drills" which focus on the building blocks of the offenses I will cover. The six skill drills (passing, dribbling, screening and backscreening, give and gos, and pick and rolls) will be essential in running an effective offense and should be practiced first.

The last component of this book will be simple offensive basketball sets. I have compiled four of my favorite and most potent basketball offenses that I have either taught or played in throughout my years in the basketball world. Many of the offenses I will cover can be built on to be incredibly intricate. They also can have specific play calls derived from their basic format making them more versatile. I won't be focusing on those in-depth topics in this book. Instead, I will key in on basic, teachable offensive sets that you can use right away with your team. While laying out the steps for these drills and offenses, I will first explain these process through text. Then, you will see several images to help walk you through it. Ideally, the offensive sets I provide can be run over and over without too much variation until your team masters them. With that being said, let's get into some basketball terminology.

Basketball Terminology

Point guard (1): The point guard is your leader and coach on the floor. Usually, they will organize and set up offensive sets as well as bring the ball up the court. They are often the shortest player, but the most important skills they need to possess are solid dribbling and passing skills. Often referred to as the "1" position.

Shooting guard (2): The shooting guard is a wing player that also possesses good dribbling and passing skills. However, they are more known to be shooters and scorers. In several basic offenses, they are placed on the right side of the floor.

Small forward (3): The small forward has skills that are normally tied to both post players and guards. They are versatile and should have decent rebounding, shooting, and dribbling skills. They often are placed on the left side of the court.

Power forward (4): Power forwards are usually one of the taller players on the floor that spend most of their time in the post. They will need to be a strong rebounder and screener with good post moves. Can be called a post player or big.

Center (5): Often the tallest player on the court, centers do not typically possess outside shooting range or other guard traits. However, they are great rebounders, low post scorers, and can defend the rim on defense. Can be called a post player or big.

Triple threat: The position in which players should catch the ball. It is a crouched/athletic stance in which the player's shooting foot is slightly backward and the ball is placed back into their shooting pocket. It is called triple threat because they can shoot, pass, or dribble out of this stance.

Wing: The wing area is located on the side of the floor near where the free throw line extended meets the three point line. Wing players are typically guards. The wing is designated as either "ballside" or "weakside."

Ballside: Referring to the wing/post where the ball handler is.

Weakside: Referring to the wing/post opposite of the ball handler.

Low Post: The lane area between/around the blocks.

High Post: The free throw line area between each elbow.

Basket cut: An offensive move by a player without the ball where they sprint towards the basket.

Flash: An offensive move by a player without the ball where they advance towards the ball.

Skip pass: Making a pass that is not to an adjacent player player on the floor. Often a skip pass goes from one side of the court to the other.

Pick and roll: An offensive play where a player sets a screen (pick) for the ball handler and then rolls to the hoop as the defender falls behind the screener and as ball handler drives to the basket.

Pick and pop: An offensive play where a player sets a screen (pick) for the ball handler and then fades away from the hoop losing the defender for an open jump shot and as ball handler drives to the basket.

Give and go: An offensive play where the ball handler makes a pass and then immediately cuts to the basket expecting a return pass.

Man to man: A defensive scheme that has players matchup and guard a single player throughout the possession.

Zone: A defensive strategy where players are responsible for players who enter their specific area (or zone) throughout a defensive possession.

Short corner: The spot on the floor between the block and the three point line on the baseline. Advantageous on offense, especially against zone defenses, because it causes the defense to collapse and opens up gaps for the offense.

Penetrate: Dribbling to the hoop or an open gap in the defense.

Paint: The area that is encapsulated in lane from free throw line to the baseline.

V-cut: An offensive move where a player fakes a basket cut, but returns toward the area where they started from.

Perimeter: The general area around the 3 point line.

Block: A low post area on the lane designated with a thick rectangle. Generally an area that post players occupy.

Elbow: The area at the corner of the free throw line and the lane. An advantageous spot for players to catch the ball offensively.

Free throw line extended: The imaginary line that exists if the free throw line where to extend to each side of the court.

Top of the key/circle: The area of the floor just above the middle of the circle that is above the free throw line.

Skill Drills

You can have all the talent in the world, but if you don't have a great foundation in the fundamental skills of basketball, you won't be as successful as you should be. The fundamentals that I'm covering in the Skill Drill portion of this book will be essential to effectively running the offensive sets we will go over later, but also to just be a quality basketball player in any offense. There are many, many drills that can be done to hone these imperative skills, but I wanted to detail standard drills that I've come to know to get you started. We will dive into the topics of:

1. Passing
2. Dribbling
3. Screening
4. Backscreening
5. Cutting or the Give and Go
6. Pick and Roll

Passing

Have your players partner up with one basketball between them. You can have them stand approximately a free throw width apart to start this drill. Once in place, they will work on the passing moves below.
- Standard two handed chest pass
- Right handed chest pass
- Left handed chest pass
- Right handed bounce pass
- Left handed bounce pass

A few tips to make the drill more effective:
- Have the pair increase their distance from each other every so often to increase difficulty.
- Make sure that each time the players catch the ball they are in triple threat position.
- Have your players make a fake pass before completing the appropriate one.

Dribbling

We can focus on a couple of drills to beef up your team's dribbling skills. The main thing in each drill is to have their eyes up and to keep them in an athletic stance. The first one is an individual drill where each player needs a basketball. Have them circle up around you and copy your lead as you spend approximately 30 seconds or so on each move below:
- Right/Left hand dribble with arm bar
- Crossover dribble
- Through the legs dribble
- Behind the back dribble
- Figure 8 dribble

Next, you can have them partner up. When this is done, have one player handle both balls doing the drills below and then switching with their partner:
- Standard two ball dribble
- High two ball dribble
- Low two ball dribble
- One high, one low two ball dribble
- Figure 8 two ball dribble (if too advanced, have them roll the ball on the ground)

Now that we have those stationary drills set up, you will want to get them to do this one on the move. You can simply use some of those same dribbling moves above along with some movement up and down the court, but also I like to do a different drill to work on some other skills. This next drill requires there to be two balls with a ball each given to the first two players in line, or each player can have a ball if possible. Players will line up along one wing and perform 3 dribble moves once to the left and once the right. They can do this series twice finishing at the rim the first time with a layup and the second time with a jump shot. Then, switch sides of the court. Here are the moves:

- Stutter step dribble
- Inside out dribble
- Crossover dribble

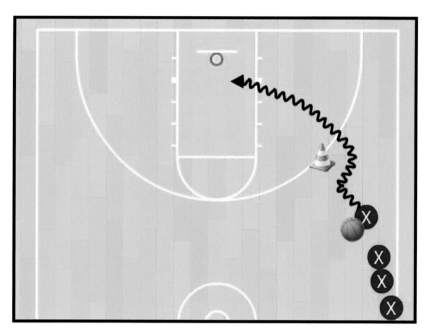

Dribbling drill from the wing

Screening

Have your players divide up into groups of three with one basketball. One player will be the passer, one will be the screener, and one will be the defender. Have the passer on one end, then spaced about five feet facing him/her, the screener, and then about five to ten feet from the screener should be the defender.

The passer will initiate the drill by slapping the ball. At this point the screener will turn and set a solid screen on the defender. A solid screen means their feet are planted shoulder width apart and that are on balance taking care not to lean one way or another. The defender will then decide to either go left or right advancing toward the passer. Once the defender makes their choice, the screener should turn and block the defender and come back to the pass for a pass. Have each player rotate through each position.

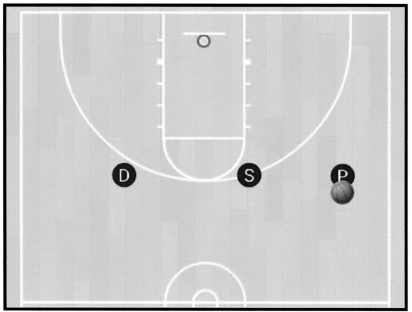

Screening drill starting positions

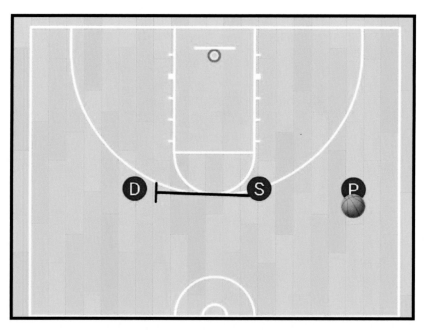

Drill starts with a pick being set by the screener

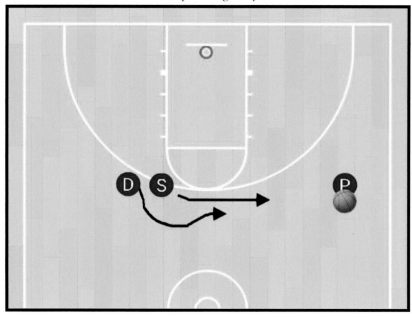

Screener rolls to the ball and the defender chases for a steal

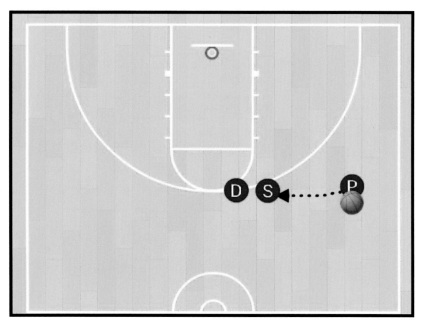

Passer makes a quality pass to the screener

Keys to emphasize:
- Passer should start in triple threat position. Make a fake pass and then complete a solid bounce or chest pass to the screener.

- Screener should set a solid screen. That means they should be balanced and not moving. When they roll, they should roll so that they are opening to the ball. That way they don't lose track of the ball. They need to finish the drill by running toward the passer and catching the ball with a jump stop in triple threat position.

- Defender should wait for the screener to arrive and do their best to get around them once they decide to go left or right without fouling.

Backscreening

For this drill, we need two lines, one at the baseline and one at a wing. The coach will stand at the opposite wing or top of the key and will be the passer in this drill.

The player at the baseline will start in the center of the lane and flash to the free throw line expecting a pass.

The coach will fake a pass and that is the queue for this player to continue to the high post on the side of his teammate to set a backscreen.

The player on the wing will fake like they are coming to the ball, but then duck under and use the backscreen. They will continue to the low post ball side and, if they receive the ball, finish a lay up. If not, he or she should continue to the corner of the floor.

If the cutter doesn't receive the ball, the screener should roll back to the opposite high post for a short jump shot.

Have these players switch lines and continue the drill.

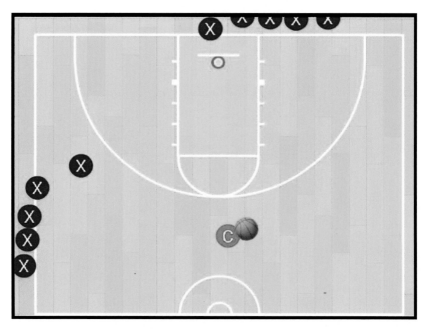

Setup to backscreening drill with two lines: baseline and wing

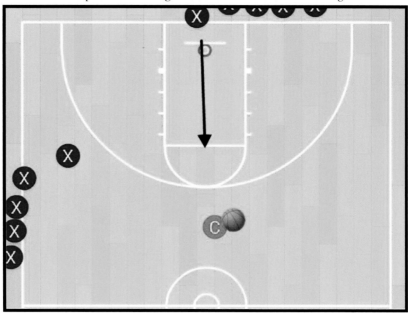

Drill begins with baseline player flashing to the free throw area

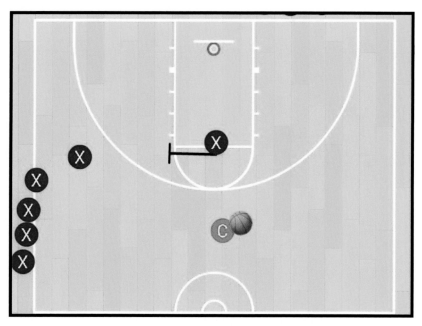

Flashing player then runs toward the wing player and sets a screen at the high post area

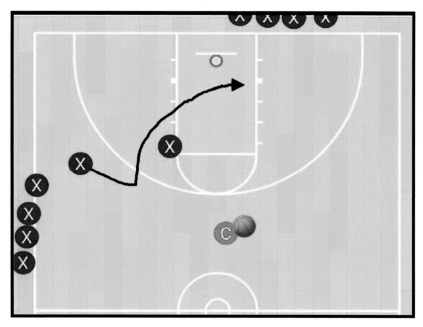

Wing player fakes like they are going over the screen but then ducks back toward the rim

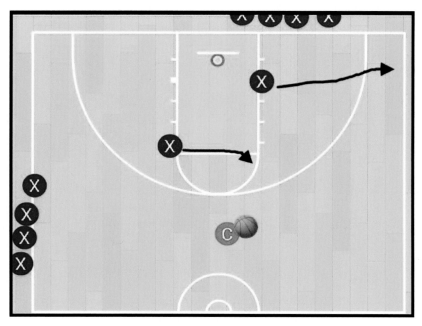

Both players then cut toward the opposite side of the floor expecting a pass

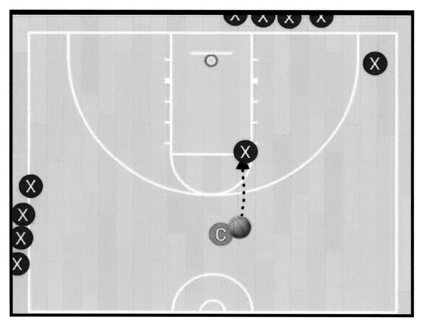

Coach finishes the drill by passing to either the backcutter or screener who attempts to score

Cutting/Give and Go

Start this drill by having your team form two lines, one at the top of the key and one on either the left or right wing. It also helps if you put a defender or chair in front of the top of the key. The player on top will start with the ball. They will make a pass to the wing then fake like they are going to go away from the pass, but instead cut in front of the chair toward the basket. The player on the wing makes a crisp bounce or chest pass so the cutter can finish with a layup. Have the players switch lines. You can also make them switch sides and have the ball start in the opposite position.

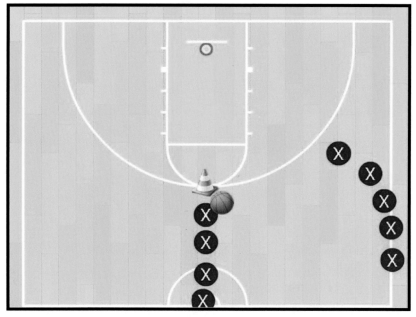

Starting formation of the give and go drill has two lines: on the wing and the top of the key

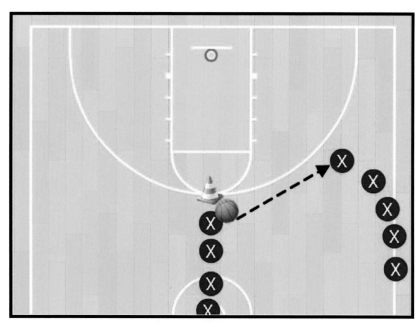

Drill begins with a pass from top of the key to the wing

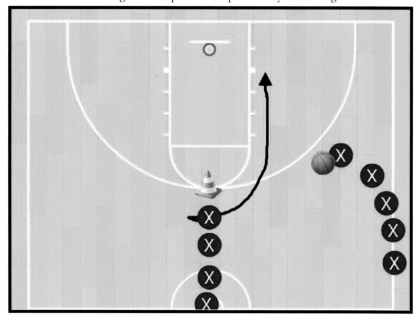

Player up top will then fake one way and then cut toward the basket in the opposite direction

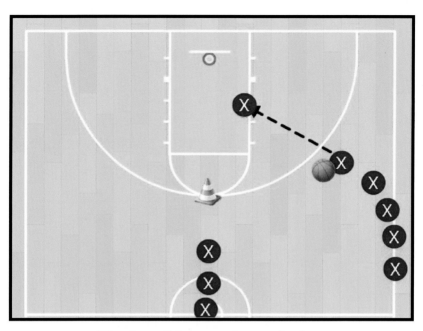

Wing player will then pass to the cutter for a layup

Pick and Roll

Begin this final skill drill with the players forming two lines, one at the wing and the other on the baseline. The ball will start on the wing. It is helpful to have a defender or chair placed in front of the line on the wing. The drill starts by having the baseline player set a solid screen on the inside shoulder of the defender. The wing player will then dribble toward the screen almost bumping into the screener's shoulder. As the wing player continues to the hoop for a shot or layup, the screener will roll to the basket by opening toward the ball and cutting to the hoop. The dribbler can finish with a layup or pass to the screener for a layup.

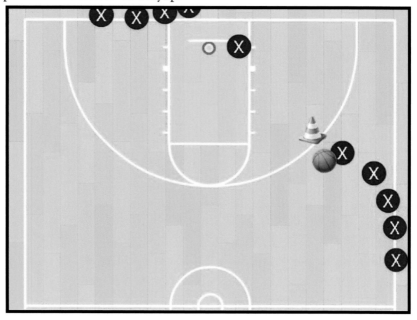

Start the pick and roll drill with two lines: on the wing and the baseline

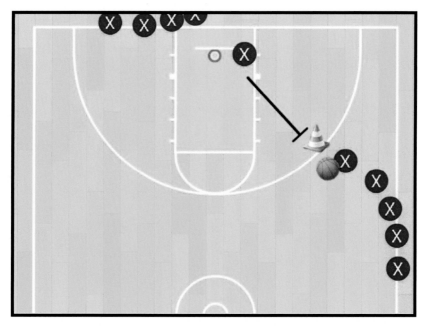

Player on the block will set a screen for the wing player

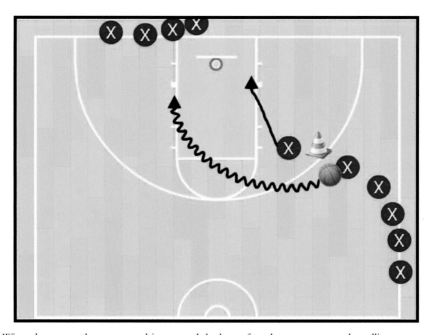

Wing player uses the screen to drive toward the hoop for a layup or pass to the rolling screener

Offensive Sets

Six skill drills later, we are ready to start installing some basic offensive strategies. I've broken this section up into four offenses. Each one will start with a short description accompanied by an overview that breaks down the type of personnel that each offense favors, the skill drills that will be helpful in running that offense, and whether the offense should be run against a zone or man defense. Then, I will walk through the various functions and options that are available in each one including pictures that will hopefully help some of the text come to life. The four offenses I will elaborate on are ones I have either used as a player or coach during various years of youth basketball. I hope they are as useful to you as they are to me. Here are the names of the offenses:

1. Seven
2. Perimeter
3. 1-4 High
4. Runner

Seven

This offense goes by many different names, but I always refer to it as "Seven" since that is how it was taught to me all throughout my years on the school basketball team. Seven is a classic, yet versatile offense. The basic set is easy to pick up, but it can have numerous playcall variations once that set is mastered.

Overview:
- Utilizes traditional personnel (2 post players and 3 wing players)
- Can be run against man or zone
- Skill drills needed: passing, dribbling, screens

Seven starts out with the two post players stationed on the wings as the point guard brings up the ball in the center of the court. The other two wing players will start on the blocks. For younger teams, you may opt to just have the wing players start on the wings instead of the blocks. Instead of the down screen, the guards on the wing would simply v-cut.

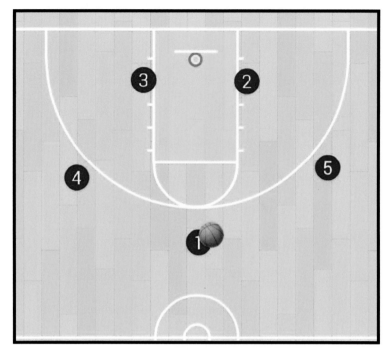

Basic starting positions of Seven

The offensive set begins when the point guard reaches just above the top of the key. At this point, the post players should set a down screen for the guards who are on the blocks. The guards will wait for the screen to arrive and then replace the post players on the wings ready to receive a pass from the point guard. It's important to have your point guard keep their head up along with their dribble. If they don't they may miss an open player or get stuck without a quality passing lane.

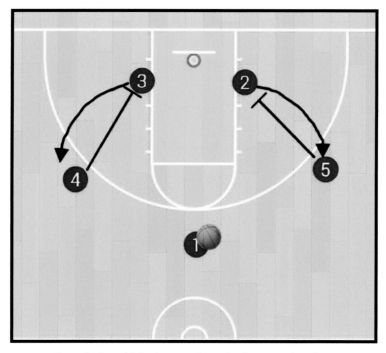

Seven begins with backscreens from the players on the wings

** Once you run this enough, the defense might make an adjustment expecting the down screens. To counteract this, they may just assume the screen is coming and have their defenders cheat above the screen knowing that you are likely to end up there. If your opponent does this, you could have the guards flash through the lane for an unexpected variation and hopefully an open shot or layup.

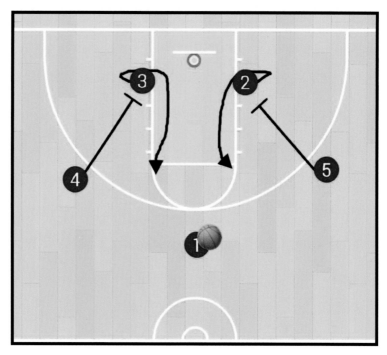

When the defense starts to cheat, have your guards mix it up

The point guard continues the set by passing it to either wing depending on which side appears to be open. The guard on the wing should catch the ball in triple threat position. They should be looking to shoot or drive to the hoop if they are open, but if not we want them to let the offense to develop.

After the point guard passes, they will screen away to the opposite wing. Likewise, the post player on the ballside, if they don't receive an entry pass right away, will screen away for the weakside post player.

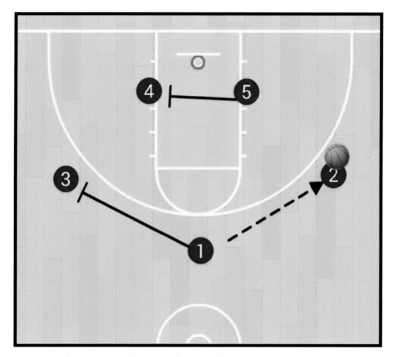

After a pass to the wing, players will screen away from the ball

The opposite side post player (4 in this example) will have two options on where to go when he/she is screened. They can either run to the opposite block or high post. The screening post player (5) will roll to the opposite spot that is not filled by the other post player.

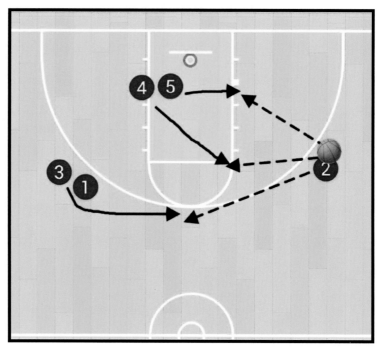

The wing player will have several options with players coming off of screens and rollers

At this point, we want to get the ball into the post if possible. If either the 4 or 5 player does get the entry pass, the other post player should dive to the opposite block. This movement will hopefully catch the defense off guard and keep adequate spacing in the paint.

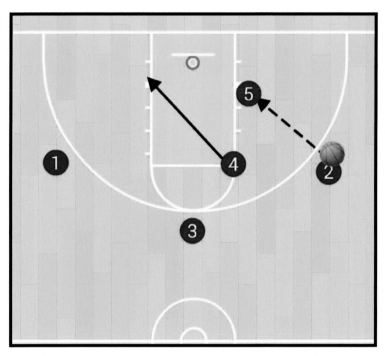

In this scenario, the low post was open so we want to work the ball inside

If the shot is not open at any point before this action, the post players can kick the ball back out to any of the wing players and run the set again. Most often, if the post player cannot get a shot, they can kick it to the opposite wing player for an open jump shot.

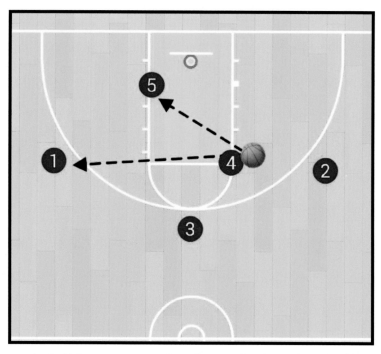

In this scenario, the high post was open and now has several options to keep the offense moving

** Just as we talked about before, the defense might get used to how this offense begins. That doesn't mean you can't shake things up to keep them on their heels. For an added wrinkle, have your wings criss cross to start the offense.

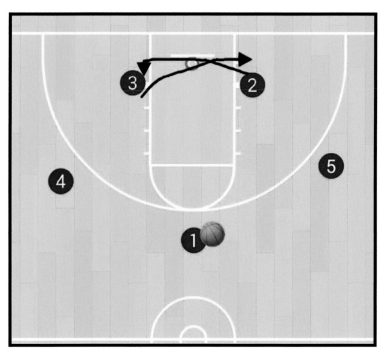

Criss crossing your wings can confuse the defense to start off Seven

Perimeter

Perimeter is a motion based offense that is great for youth basketball because it essentially is a series of rules that you can customize depending on the skill and experience of your team. You can also build on the basics over time.

Overview:
- Features 4 players stationed around the perimeter and 1 post player
- Provides ideal spacing and almost constant movement to stretch defenses
- Adjustable based on your team's skill
- Skill drills needed: passing, dribbling, give and go, screens, pick and roll, backscreens

To set up the Perimeter offense, we need to layout the specific spots that players will rotate through. There are four perimeter spots (blue) that the 4 perimeter players will shuffle through. There are also four spots (red) that the 1 post player will rotate through. You can see the locations we want our team in the next diagram:

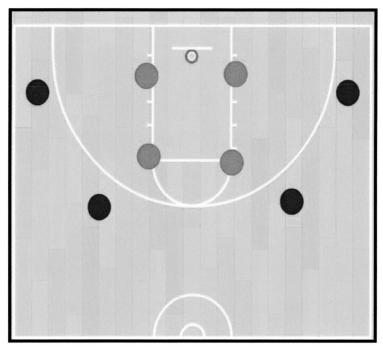

Red spots represent your post positions and blue represent the wing positions

Normally, when the offense first starts I will designate my team to start in the spots shown in the next diagram:

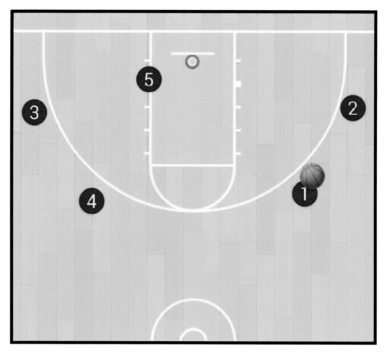

Spacing in the Perimeter offense opens up chances for cuts and drives

Now, let's break down the 3 basic rules for this offense and see how they play out on the floor.

Rule 1 (post player) - Flash to the spot closest to the ball immediately.

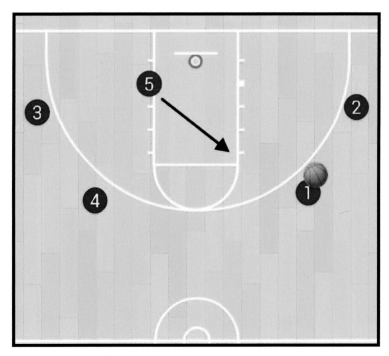

Player 5 here cuts to the high post for an entry pass

In this case, the post player will flash to the high post nearest to the point guard as he/she brings the ball up the floor.

Rule 2 (perimeter players) - If you pass the ball to a perimeter spot immediately adjacent to you, you must make a basket cut.

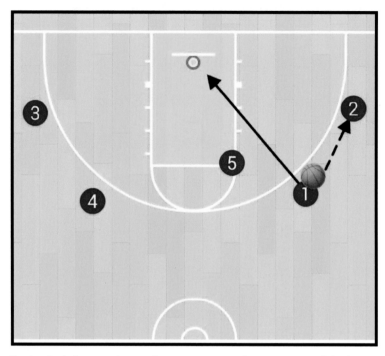

Passing the ball to a perimeter player next to your triggers an automatic basket cut

Rule 3 (perimeter players) - If there is a spot that is adjacent to the ball open, you must fill it.

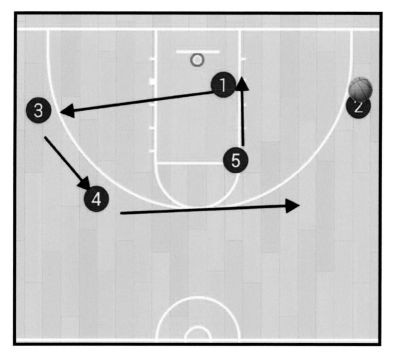

Filling the spot next to you causes a chain reaction of movement

For less experienced or younger teams, this might be all the rules you can install for a while until they master them. The important things to emphasize is that every time the ball moves, players receiving it should look first to make a quick pass or attempt to score by shooting or driving to the rim.

To continue building on these three foundational rules, let's add some more.

Rule 4 (perimeter players) - If the ball enters the high post, the lower wing spots will cut and replace each other.

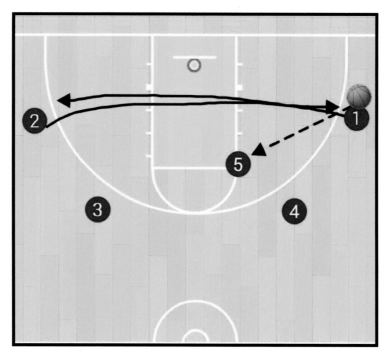

When the ball enters the high post, this offense is the most dangerous

Rule 5 (perimeter players) - If the ball enters the low post, the opposite low wing player cuts to the weakside block. If the ball is passed out the the perimeter, they retreat back to their spot.

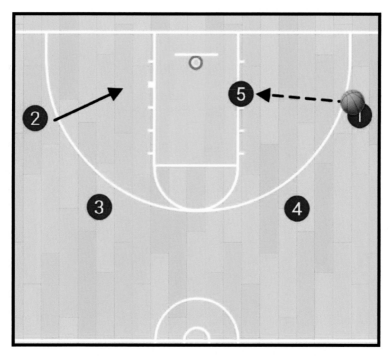

Weakside defenders might fall asleep, so look for the cut here

Rule 6 (perimeter/post players) - If the ball is skipped, the post player will set a screen on the player receiving the skip pass. This initiates a pick and roll situation.

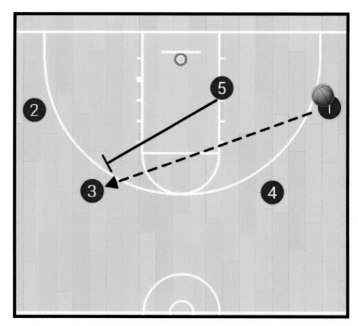

Skipping the ball initiates a pick and roll

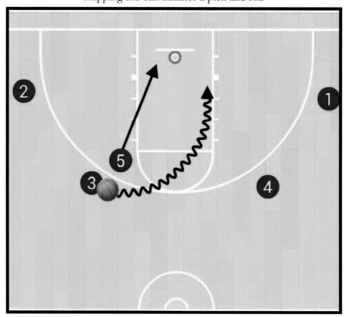

Pick and rolls can put a lot of pressure on the defense and lead to open shots

Rule 7 (perimeter players) - If the ball is dribbled at you, make a basket cut.

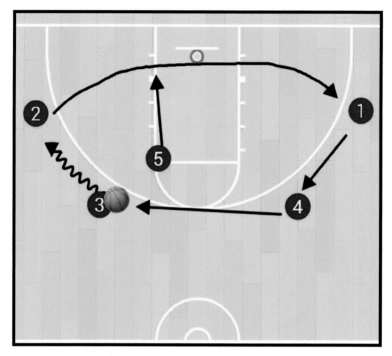

Cutting to the basket causes a massive rotation

Rule 8 (perimeter/post player) - If the ball is passed back out to the perimeter by the post player, he/she must set a screen on the player receiving the ball. This initiates a pick and roll situation.

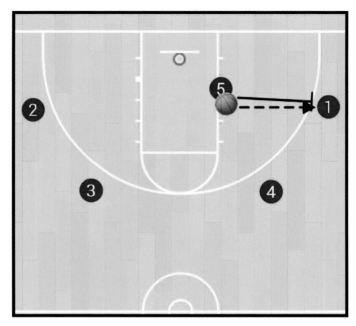

Getting the ball back to the perimeter sets up another great pick and roll opportunity

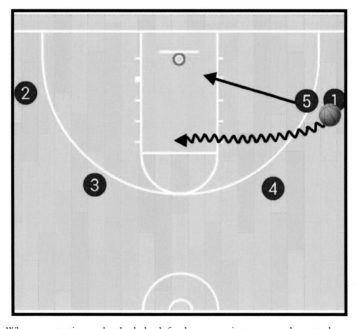

When penetrating make the help defenders commit to you or else get a layup

You can see how this offense can become complex quickly. After these first eight rules, you could even add more, but this should be more than enough to make this offense unpredictable and effective.

1-4 High

The 1-4 High offense (sometimes called 14) can have a seemingly endless amount of variations similar to the Seven offense I walked through earlier. The idea is to bring your players away from the basket to allow for open back cuts and open lanes for effective pick and rolls/pick and pops.

Overview:
- Traditional personnel offense (3 guards, 2 post players)
- Emphasis on pick and roll game as well as backdoor cuts
- Effective against man to man or zone defenses
- Skill drills needed: passing, dribbling, screens, cutting, pick and roll

For youth basketball coaches, the 1-4 High offense has two imperative variations that should be run first before building off of its versatility. Let's start with the basic format of the offense and then I will dive into each variation.

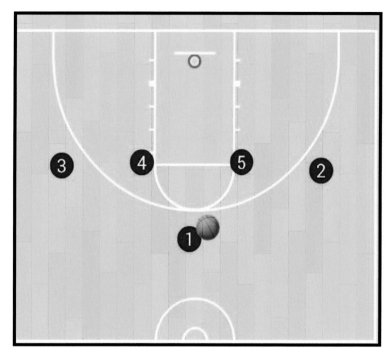

1-4 High opens up the area close to the rim

Above, you can see why this offensive set is called 1-4 High. There is one player (your point guard) up top. Then at the free line height area, you have your four other players spread out with the two post players at the high post and the other two guards on the wings.

The first variation of the offense occurs when the point guard makes a pass to either wing player. In this case, the offense will focus on using pick and rolls to score. However, the first action that occurs after the pass is a basket cut by the guard up top after passing. The weakside wing player will replace the cutting guard.

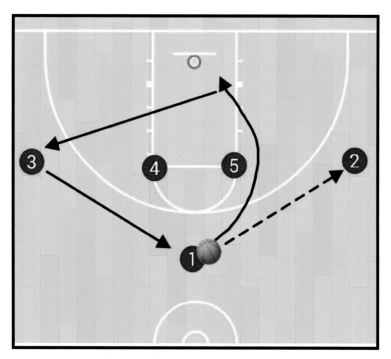

Passing to the wing allows for an instant cut and screen action

If the cutter does not receive the ball, the post player on the side of the floor that receives the ball will set a screen on the wing defender.

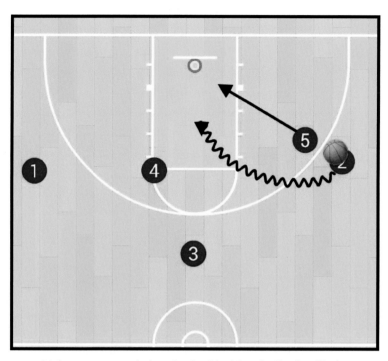

It's important to reach the paint for this pick and roll to be effective

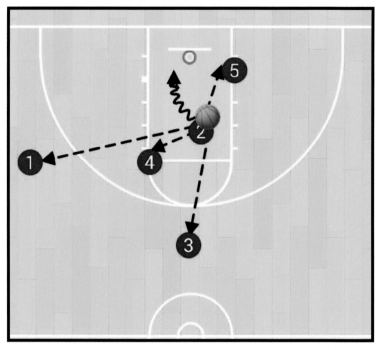

Once you reach the paint, a myriad of options open up

This action gives the wing player several options to choose from:
- Dribble drive to the rim for a layup or stop for a jump shop
- Pass to the opposite high post where the other post player can make a scoring move
- Kick the ball up to the top of the key for an outside shot
- Hit the rolling post player for a layup
- Pass it to the weakside wing player for an outside shot

If this action is well defended, you can simply begin the action again by passing the ball to a wing player and starting the motion all over.

The second aspect of the 1-4 High offensive set is initiated when the ball is entered to the high post. Once this happens, the wing player that is on the ballside will immediately back cut to hopefully catch their defender napping.

Simultaneously, the post player will dive to the basket. The other two wing players will rotate to allow for proper spacing if this initially unsuccessful.

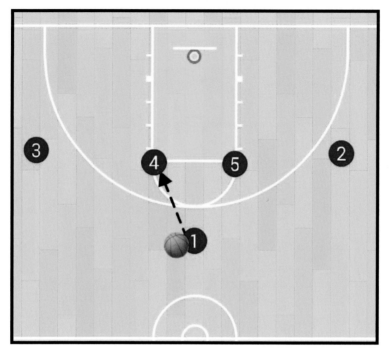

The second option of the 1-4 High offense starts with an entry pass to the post

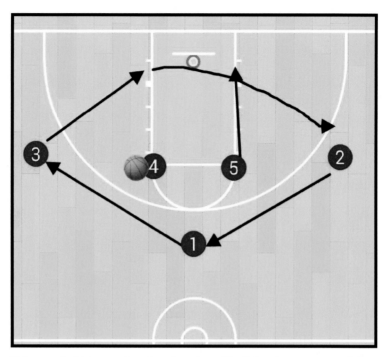

Make sure the high post player here is patient with all the movement around them

Runner

Zone offenses typically have a couple of distinct weaknesses including offensive rebounds, effective shooting, and quick passing. The Runner offense tries to emphasize those three aspects.

Overview:
- Zone offense that works best odd zone fronts (1-3-1, 2-3, or 3-2 zones)
- Places the best shooter in a position to run the baseline
- Often overloads one side of the floor in order to gain an advantage
- Skill drills needed: passing, dribbling, and backscreens

Let's take a look at the basic layout of the Runner offense:

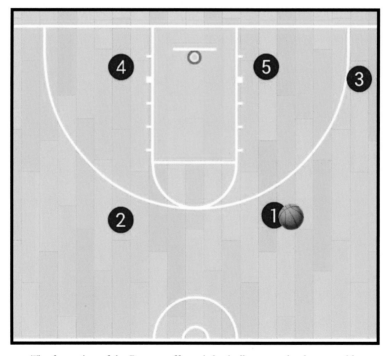

The formation of the Runner offense is basically an overload to one side

The runner's (3) job is to patrol the baseline, following where the ball is on the court. The post players will also try to assist in getting the runner open by setting backscreens. This is the basic motion of the offense as the ball is reversed by the guards up top.

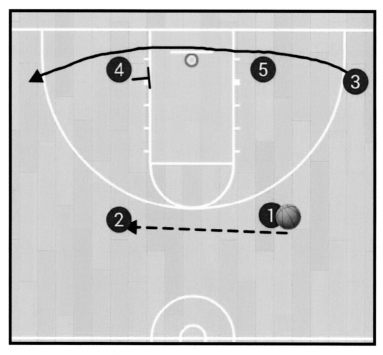

Your runner should have excellent looks to shoot

As the two guards who are up top are reversing the ball, they should be looking to pass the ball on the wing to the runner or looking for the post players to be open in the paint. If the ball does end up in the runner's hands on the wing, the post players will overload the ballside of the court. This happens when the weakside post player flashes to the elbow or block depending on what spot is open.

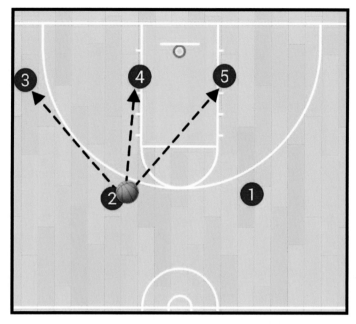

Don't forget to feed the post

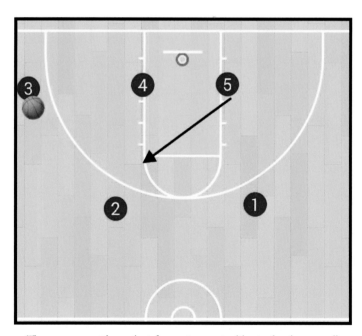

The runner must be patient for post opportunities to develop as well

If there is no openings for a shot, drive, or pass into the post, the runner can kick the ball back up to the guards for a reversal pass. In that case, the post players will revert to their starting positions and flash when it is received on the other wing.

It's imperative for passes to be quick and for players to utilize fake passes to move the defense out of position as much as possible.

Thanks for Reading!

With that, we have reached the end of my offensive strategies for coaching youth basketball. I hope this book was an enlightening and helpful read for teaching your team the necessary terms, skills, and offensive strategies to be successful and have a good time this basketball season. Do remember to keep experimenting! As I mentioned before, these offenses can be built upon with new wrinkles or one time plays that are run out of their formations. As you continue to master the offenses, more opportunities will open up to your team. Best of luck and thank you for reading.

Note From the Author: Reviews are a game winning buzzer beater to authors like me! If you've enjoyed this book, would you consider rating it and reviewing it on www.Amazon.com?

Made in the USA
Columbia, SC
24 May 2017